Using Science TO PLAY BASEBALL

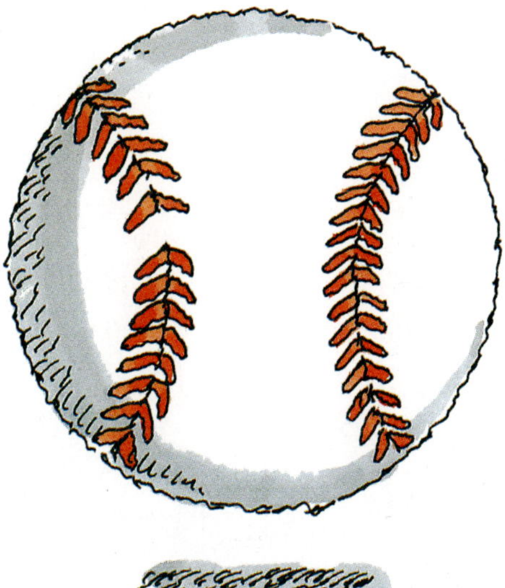

written by Emily North
illustrated by Jared D. Lee

McGraw-Hill School Division
New York Farmington

Do you want to learn about baseball? Before you ask your coach, you might want to talk to a scientist.

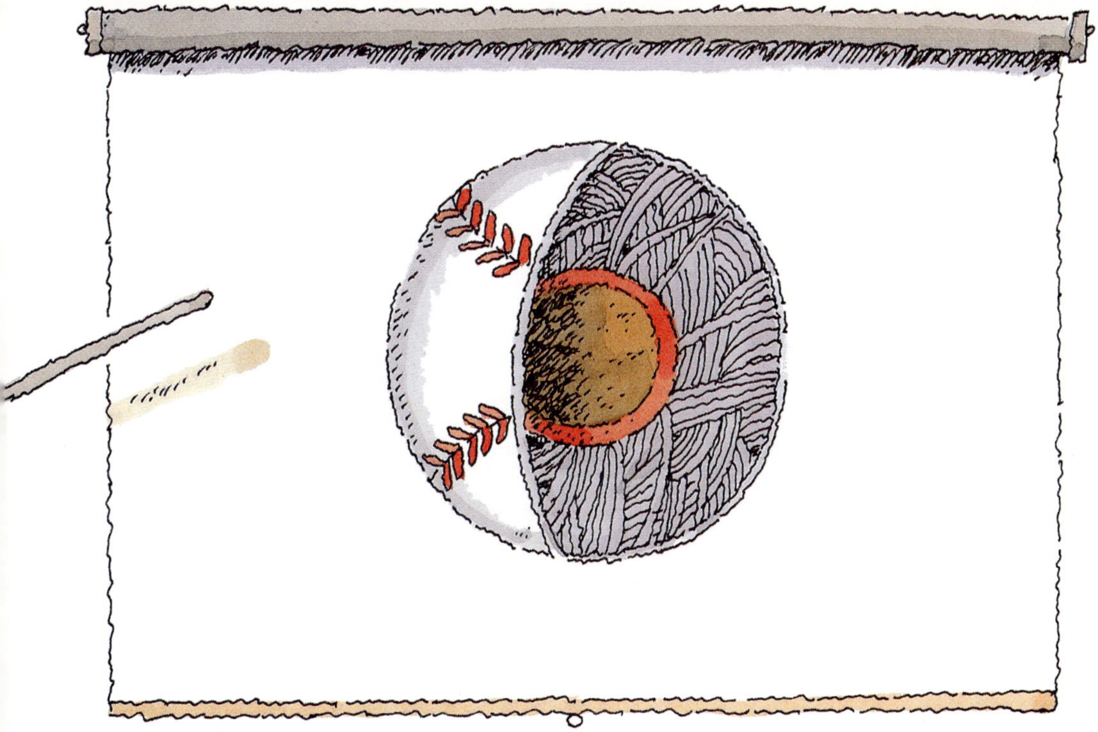

Why Is a Baseball a Baseball?

Baseballs are made of yarn wound tightly around a piece of cork or rubber, then covered with leather. They weigh 5 to 5 1/4 ounces and are about nine inches in diameter. A baseball is much smaller and harder than a basketball, but bigger than a golf ball. A smaller, more tightly wound object contains more energy. Imagine you had two sponges, one the size of a beach ball, the other the size of a golf ball. If you pressed them both down to the size of a pea, which one would spring back faster to its original shape?

That's right—the bigger one. The more matter that's packed into a small space, the more potential energy you have.

The outside of a baseball is white leather stitched together with red cotton thread. The stitching on the surface of the baseball helps the ball cut through the air at a faster rate. A smooth object has a harder time moving through the air flow around it, and goes a lot slower than something with a rough surface. That is why golf balls have little dimples all over them.

How Does the Bat Help You Hit?

The baseball bat used in the major leagues is made of ash wood. It weighs between 31 and 36 ounces, and is about 36 inches long.

A heavy bat will build up more energy as it swings, but it also requires more time to follow through and hit the ball.

A light bat doesn't hit the ball as hard, but you can swing it a lot faster. This way you can wait longer before you swing and get a better idea of where the ball is going.

The speed of the ball can also help you know what type of equipment to use. Heavy bats work better against faster balls, but a lighter bat is better for more slowly pitched balls. Try to find out if you're hitting against a fast pitcher or a slow pitcher before you pick your bat!

How Does the Ball Change Direction?

The stitching on the ball can change the direction of the pitch!

The stitches cut through the air better and help the ball move faster, so the ball will move more quickly in the direction that the stitches are facing. If the ball is pitched with the stitches facing first base, the ball will head that way.

But pitchers can throw the ball in special ways that will make the ball spin in another direction as it heads toward home plate. This means that the ball that looked like it was heading toward first base will suddenly turn and curve toward third! The batter will make a mistake and swing in the wrong direction.

Slowly pitched balls will pick up this curve a lot more easily, but then the batter will see the ball change direction. A fast-pitched ball will have less time to curve away, but the change will be almost invisible. The batter won't be able to see it coming.

By the way, some of those curve balls look like they go two feet from the center line. But no curve ball ever strays more than a few inches from the center line. It's just a trick of the eye!

What About Hitting?

Most of the force that goes into hitting the ball comes from the motion of the player's body as he or she swings. As the body rotates and moves toward the ball, the energy from this movement is transferred to the arms. The arms and hands don't supply the energy—they just guide it to the bat. Then this energy goes through the bat as it hits the ball and WHAM—there it goes!

Now, since the arms only transfer the energy, you may be surprised to find out that it doesn't really help a right-handed batter to hit right-handed. In fact, there are lots of reasons why it is better to hit left-handed.

The left-handed batter is facing first base, so he or she is ready to run after the ball is hit, and

right field fences are usually closer than left field fences, so it is easier to hit a home run if you are a left-handed batter swinging toward right field. And there are more right-handed pitchers, which means they are pitching on an easy-to-hit slant to the left-handed batter. So even if you are right-handed, you might want to try batting left-handed.

How Far Can You Hit a Ball?

If a ball is pitched at 85 miles per hour, and a batter swings at 86 miles per hour, then the perfectly hit ball will travel about 450 feet. But other things can affect the distance the ball travels and how well you perform.

If the ball is pitched at 95 miles per hour, you can add another 10 feet, so the perfectly hit ball will travel 460 feet.

If the batter pulls toward the foul line instead of dead center, the ball will pick up another 15 feet. Now we're at 475 feet.

On a hot, dry day, maybe at 100 degrees in July, the air is thinner and the ball can move faster, so add another 10 feet, for a total of 485 feet.

Hot weather makes the ball more "lively," which means it is more elastic and can go farther. Add another 10 feet for the lively ball and you're at 495 feet.

What if there is a 10 mile per hour wind behind the batter? Then the ball will go 40 more feet, and now the ball has traveled 535 feet!

And if this game happens to be taking place in Denver, well, then the ball park is higher, and the air is thinner yet, and you can add another 40 feet.

All of those possibilities were thought out by scientists. Now baseball players everywhere have accepted these beliefs, and use them when they play and when they plan strategy. So no matter how talented a player you are, knowing more about science will help you know more about baseball!